ASTRONOMY

Carole Stott

KINGFISHER

BOSTON

KINGFISHER

a Houghton Mifflin Company imprint
222 Berkeley Street
Boston, Massachusetts 02116
www.houghtonmifflinbooks.com

First published by in 2003
10 9 8 7 6 5 4 3 2 1

1TR/0703/GCUP/MA(MA)/140NMA

LIBRARY OF CONGRESS CATALOGING-IN-PUBLICATION DATA
Stott, Carole.
Astronomy/by Carole Stott—1st ed.
p. cm.
Includes index.
Summary: Discusses famous astronomers, the solar system, the stars,
and other aspects of astronomy.
1. Astronomy—Juvenile literature. [1. Astronomy.] I. Title.

QB46.S9515 2003
520—dc21   2002043317

ISBN 0-7534-5582-X

Editor: Catherine Brereton
Coordinating editor: Caitlin Doyle
Designer: Mark Bristow
Consultant: Dr. Margaret Penston, Institute of Astronomy,
University of Cambridge (for the Royal Astronomical Society)
Indexer: Sue Lightfoot
Senior production controllers: Nancy Roberts, Lindsey Scott
DTP manager: Sarah Pfitzner
DTP operator: Primrose Burton
Picture research: Rachael Swann
Artwork archivists: Wendy Allison, Jenny Lord
Cover design by Mike Davis

Printed in China

The Publisher would like to thank the **Royal
Astronomical Society** for their help and
cooperation in the production of this book.

Since its formation in 1820 the fellows of the
Royal Astronomical Society have worked to
advance astronomy and geophysics through
frontline scientific research. The Society gives
grants for scientific work and distributes results
throughout the world—at meetings, by the written
word, and on the web. The Society provides
information and advice to young people who
are thinking of becoming astronomers or
geophysicists and to their teachers.

Further information about the Society can be
obtained from its web site: **www.ras.org.uk**

CONTENTS

LOOKING AT THE UNIVERSE

From Earth we can look out into the universe. People have always done this. Many have enjoyed the splendor of a starry sky or gazed in wonder at the brilliant Moon. Others have done more than wonder and have investigated what these places are like. The scientific study of the stars and planets is called astronomy, and the men and women who do this work are called astronomers. Astronomers reveal the universe's fascinating sights and intriguing worlds for everyone to understand and enjoy. They also explain how everything fits together and how the universe changes with time. They have even pieced together its past and predicted its future.

Studying the universe

Unlike other scientists, who are able to get close to what they study, astronomers have to work at a long distance. They use a range of tools and techniques to study the stars and planets from Earth. Their most fundamental tool is the telescope. Yet there is a lot to see with the eye alone. Take your first step toward becoming an astronomer by simply looking up and into the universe.

What is the universe?

The universe is everything that exists. That means Earth, everything on Earth, and everything that surrounds our planet. It includes the smallest particles and the largest galaxies, frozen planets, explosive stars, holes in space, and life itself. Everything in the universe is made up of the same chemical elements that we find on Earth, and the laws of science that operate on Earth also govern the entire universe.

Looking up

Professional astronomers use powerful telescopes kept in mountaintop observatories (left). Amateur astronomers use their eyes, binoculars, or a portable telescope (right).

Galaxies

Astronomers are discovering new things all the time. At the beginning of the 1900s we only knew about one galaxy. Now we know there are billions of them, including the Sombrero (top) and M33 (right).

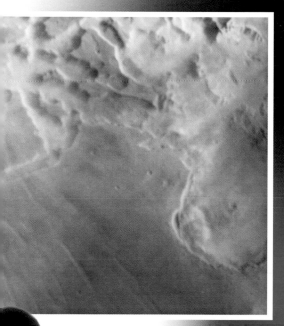

Planets

For more than 40 years astronomers have used space probes to work in space on their behalf. These probes have shown views of the planets that are not possible from Earth, like this image of the surface of Mars (above).

The Moon

By studying Earth's relationship with the Moon, astronomers learned that gravity is universal. Everything in the universe has gravity and is affected by it.

Earth

By investigating the universe around us we learn more about our home planet, Earth. We have learned about its past, present, and future.

Earth's eye view

Look up from Earth at a cloudless sky and you are looking out into the universe. Whichever way you look there are stars. In the daytime sky just one is visible—its light illuminates our sky, and it outshines all of the other stars. It is the Sun. The Sun is so close that you should never look at it directly. Its bright light can damage our eyes. At night we see a sky full of even more distant stars. Each one appears attached to a backdrop that moves with time. The Moon and planets travel across the starry background. Occasionally a passing visitor, such as a comet, adds to the view.

Starry sky
Exactly what you can see of the universe depends on where you look from, the direction you look in, the date, and the time. In all cases the most common object you'll see is a star. Each one is a star in our Milky Way galaxy. A bright milky path across your sky means that you are looking toward the heart of the galaxy.

Star patterns
The brightest stars in the night sky make up the constellation patterns. Stars differ not only in brightness but also in color, size, and distance. A red supergiant marks a shoulder of Orion, the hunter—and the Orion Nebula, a giant cloud of gas and dust, is the sword hanging from his belt of stars.

Close-up view

The Moon is the closest space object to Earth and is easily seen in our sky. By just using our eyes we can make out features on its surface. With binoculars or a telescope we can see much more. Larger and more distant objects, such as planets and galaxies, appear much smaller than the Moon but are easy to see. Their details are revealed to us through telescopes both based on Earth and in space.

The Moon and planets

Neither the Moon nor the planets have light of their own, instead they shine by reflected sunlight. They are always seen within a particular strip of sky that circles around Earth. This sky band is made up of 12 constellations collectively called the zodiac. The Moon and planets travel across the backdrop of the zodiac, constellation after constellation. The band circles around us, roughly above Earth's equator. Wherever you are on Earth you can look toward the zodiac band to see the Moon and planets.

The earliest astronomers

The first people to look up at the sky and wonder what they saw were the earliest astronomers. These observers, watching the sky thousands of years ago, drew imaginary pictures about the stars, identified five "wandering stars" (planets), and used the movements of the Sun and the Moon across the sky for keeping track of time. Whether in Europe, Africa, or Asia, they created myths and stories about the sky and what was in it. There was a lot they did not know about the universe, and what they did not understand they were often afraid of.

Fear of the unknown
Ancient Chinese astronomers recorded several comets and eclipses. But the sudden appearance of a comet or the darkening of the Sun during an eclipse caused real fear. They believed a dragon was trying to eat the Sun. Drums and gongs were banged and arrows were shot into the sky to scare the dragon away.

Egyptian universe
The ancient Egyptians believed that their sky goddess, Nut, arched over Earth. Her body was made of stars and appeared in our sky as the path of the Milky Way. Nut was held up by Shu, the god of light and air. Below them was Nut's husband, Geb, the god of Earth.

First observatories

Over the centuries astronomers began to make sense of what they saw. They made regular observations, took measurements, listed the stars, and explained how parts of the known universe fit together. Buildings and monuments were built for astronomical use. The Mayan people built the Caracol Temple in Mexico (above left) around one thousand years ago. Its windows are positioned so that Venus can be seen through them on special dates.

Calendar

Many peoples developed calendars based on the daily and yearly movement of the Sun in the sky and the changing shape of the Moon. The Aztecs, living in Central America around 500 years ago, had their own accurate calendar. Their Sun god is in the center, and the days are carved around him.

Spread of knowledge

People living in different parts of the world worked independently to learn about the universe. The Babylonians, living in the Near East more than 4,000 years ago, had the most advanced astronomical knowledge of ancient times. They knew little compared to today's astronomers, but our present knowledge can be traced back to their beginnings. The work of the Babylonians was built on by the ancient Greeks, and this was then developed and passed on to medieval Europe by Arabic-speaking peoples.

Measuring

Around 200 B.C. the Greek astronomer Eratosthenes measured the size of Earth. He compared the way sunlight struck the ground at Syrene and at Alexandria in Egypt at the same time on the summer solstice. He then used his findings to figure out the distance around Earth.

The center of the universe

Astronomers of the ancient world believed that Earth was the center of the universe and that the Sun and other objects traveled around it. These beliefs and other astronomical knowledge were collected together in a book called *Almagest* by the Greek astronomer Claudius Ptolemy, who lived in the A.D. 300s. Ptolemy's view of the universe was accepted until the 1500s when a revolutionary idea changed astronomers' minds. Nicolaus Copernicus developed a new explanation of how the known universe fit together. He believed that the Sun was at its center. Later astronomers agreed and proved him right.

Revolutionary thinking
Copernicus' belief that Earth and the other planets moved around the Sun was presented in his book *De Revolutionibus Orbium Coelestium* in 1543. Its publication marked a turning point in our understanding of the universe.

Changing ideas

For thousands of years astronomers thought the universe contained a lot less than it really does. They knew about Earth, its Moon, and five other planets—Mercury, Venus, Mars, Jupiter, and Saturn. They believed that Earth stood still while the Sun, Moon, and planets circled around it and that a sphere of stars marked the edge of the universe. This idea was replaced by Copernicus' system, which contained the same parts but explained the Sun as fixed while everything circled around it. This matched what astronomers saw in the sky. The Danish astronomer Tycho Brahe spent 20 years making detailed observations, and the German astronomer Johannes Kepler used these observations to explain the paths (orbits) of the known planets around the Sun.

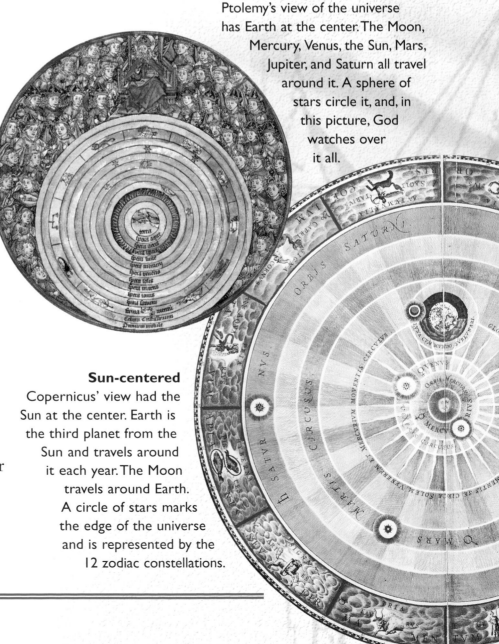

Earth-centered
Ptolemy's view of the universe has Earth at the center. The Moon, Mercury, Venus, the Sun, Mars, Jupiter, and Saturn all travel around it. A sphere of stars circle it, and, in this picture, God watches over it all.

Sun-centered
Copernicus' view had the Sun at the center. Earth is the third planet from the Sun and travels around it each year. The Moon travels around Earth. A circle of stars marks the edge of the universe and is represented by the 12 zodiac constellations.

Johannes Kepler

Kepler explained that planets orbit in ellipses, not circles. He showed that each planet moves fastest close to the Sun and slower farther away and that more distant planets orbit at slower speeds.

The universe today

Astronomers in the past believed they could see the whole universe. In fact they only saw a tiny fraction of it— only the parts they could see with their eyes. Today we know there is much more, and we know it is not centered around the Sun. The Sun is just one of the billions of stars that make up the Milky Way galaxy. The Milky Way is just one of billions of galaxies in the universe. Wherever we look there are galaxies, and if we could look at the universe from another galaxy, the view would be just the same.

Tycho Brahe

Tycho Brahe was an amazing observer who accurately measured the positions of stars and planets. He developed and used special measuring instruments such as his astronomical quadrant.

Looking closer

Starry Messenger
Galileo Galilei published his discoveries about the planets, moons, and stars in a book called *Starry Messenger* (1610). It was a sensation and made him famous. More importantly, his observations showed what momentous discoveries were possible using the telescope and how such discoveries could change the course of astronomical history.

For centuries people thought they could see the whole universe and that our planet with its moon was unique. In the early 1600s astronomers started using the newly invented telescope to look up at the sky. From 1609 Italian Galileo Galilei studied the Moon, the planets, and the stars. He detected four moons circling Jupiter, found that the Milky Way is packed full of stars, and that Venus has phases like the Moon. Over the next three centuries astronomers discovered more of the universe, learned what stars are made of, and started piecing together the story of the universe and everything in it.

Collecting light

Early telescopes were refractors, which means they used lenses to collect light. Soon the reflector, which uses mirrors, was developed. From 1666 English scientist Isaac Newton experimented with light and mirrors. He made a reflecting telescope and showed how a glass prism (right) can be used to split light into a spectrum—a rainbow band of seven colors. Today instruments called spectroscopes allow astronomers to split starlight into spectra and identify the chemical elements in a star.

First telescopes

The very first telescopes, such as the one Galileo used, were about as powerful as a pair of simple binoculars today. A lens at the sky end of a tube collected light. This was directed down the tube to the eyepiece where a smaller lens formed the light into an image of the object observed.

Biggest telescope

Herschel built increasingly powerful reflectors. His 39-ft.-long telescope (below), in use from 1789, was the biggest and most powerful telescope of its day. It had a mirror measuring 3.9 ft. in diameter.

Tracking the stars

Astronomers in the 1700s concentrated on measuring the positions of objects in the sky. Most of the cataloging and mapping was done at national observatories. Amateur astronomers also played their part. William Herschel took up astronomy as a hobby but became one of the most famous astronomers of all time. He was an excellent observer and an outstanding instrument maker. He would systematically sweep his telescopes across the sky, helped by his sister Caroline who recorded many of his observations. Herschel discovered the planet Uranus in 1781. He also discovered around 2,500 star clusters, nebulae, and galaxies.

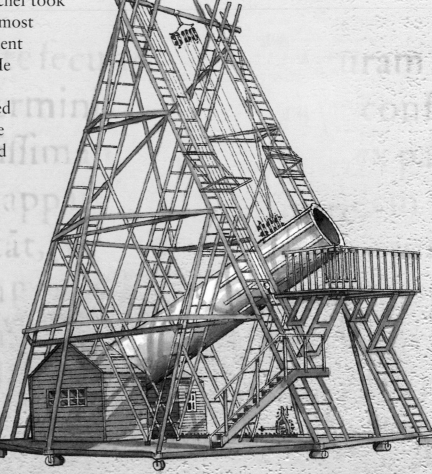

Moon watching

Galileo saw mountains on the Moon and what he thought were seas. Today we know that the Moon is dry, but we still use Galileo's name *mare* (Latin for "sea") for the large, smooth basins on the Moon's surface. These two drawings appeared in his book *Starry Messenger*.

Astronomer at work

Astronomers have been gazing up at the sky and trying to make sense of the universe for thousands of years. Over the centuries they have made astonishing discoveries and answered many questions, but there is always more to investigate. Most of the 8,000 or so professional astronomers studying the universe today work in universities around the world. Others work in government-run organizations and space agencies. They collect information from space and spend their time processing and interpreting it. Their work helps us understand and enjoy the universe around us.

Stellar astronomer
American Annie Jump Cannon started work at Harvard College Observatory in Massachusetts in 1896. Astronomers were then working hard to understand the nature of stars. Cannon studied the spectra of over 250,000 stars. She developed a system of grouping the stars into types according to their spectra. Her system is still used today.

Space astronomers
Since the 1950s astronomers have been designing and launching spacecraft to help with their work. Astronomers from the U.S. and Europe work together using data collected by the Hubble Space Telescope.

Cosmologist

Englishman Fred Hoyle (above) was one of the most important astronomers of the 1900s. One of his greatest achievements was showing how chemical elements are produced inside of stars. He also worked to explain the state of the universe. He didn't believe that the universe began in an explosion, but he did come up with the name "big bang."

Different types of astronomers

Astronomers who lived and worked more than 100 years ago studied every object and feature of the universe. The 21st-century astronomer is usually a specialist who studies just a fraction of it in great detail. Stellar astronomers are interested in the stars and what lies between them. Other astronomers concentrate on galaxies or on the solar system. Some are not concerned with objects but specialize in the different forms of information we receive such as radio or X-ray waves. Cosmologists study the origin, evolution, and future of the universe.

Astrophotographers

Astronomy and technology have always worked hand in hand. Astronomers not only design and build instruments, but they are quick to use the instruments and techniques of others. They have been taking astronomical photographs since the mid-1800s, soon after photography was invented. Today astrophotographers spend their working lives producing even better images of the sky and the objects in it. Here David Malin prepares to make an image using the 12.8 ft. Anglo-Australian telescope. His photograph of the Orion Nebula is shown behind.

Tools of the trade

Astronomers want to get the clearest and most detailed view possible of the stars and planets. For centuries they relied on their eyes alone to explore the skies. But since the invention of telescopes they have used these instruments to look even farther into space. Telescopes allow astronomers to see things bigger and more clearly. Like the human eye, they gather the light from a planet and process it into an image. But the lenses and mirrors they use gather much more light and produce a much more detailed image than our eyes are able to. Today's telescopes are enormous structures kept inside of buildings several stories high. They take years to design and build and are very expensive, each costing billions of dollars. Organizations, such as universities, or whole countries join together to share the cost and use of a telescope.

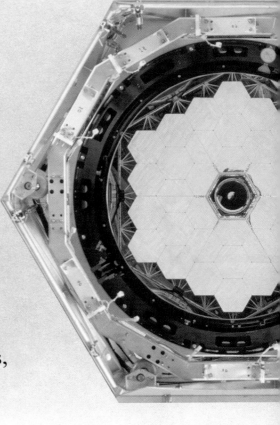

Segmented mirrors
The Keck telescopes each have a mirror measuring 32.8 ft. in diameter. They are made up of 36 hexagonal segments, each measuring 5.9 ft. across.

The Kecks
Inside of these domes are the Keck telescopes. Keck I has been used since 1993 and its twin, Keck II, since 1996. They are each around 82 ft. tall and weigh around 300 tons.

The Subaru
The telescopes on Mauna Kea are owned and run by countries around the world. The Japanese Subaru telescope (right) can be seen inside of its cylindrical dome.

Reflecting telescopes

The world's most powerful telescopes are reflectors, which use mirrors to collect light. The bigger and better a reflector's main mirror, the more light it collects and the more information we have. The first reflectors had mirrors that could fit inside of your hand. Today's are several feet across. But very large mirrors bend under their own weight. The latest telescope designs use a collection of smaller mirrors arranged together to work like one big mirror. This technique means that telescopes with mirrors many feet across can be made. Astronomers can also use individual telescopes linked together to work like a single telescope with one very large mirror.

Very Large Telescope

On a mountaintop in Paranal, Chile, four separate telescopes have mirrors 26.9 ft. across. Together they are known as the VLT (the Very Large Telescope). Each telescope is one billion times more powerful than the human eye. When linked together by computer, they are even more powerful.

City of domes

A mountaintop observatory is usually home to a number of large telescopes. Mauna Kea, a dormant volcano in Hawaii, has 12 world-class telescopes on its site, including the two Kecks, which are jointly the world's largest individual telescopes. Astronomers using the instruments do not work at the eyepiece of the telescopes. They are usually found farther down the mountain, where they use a television system and computers to record information collected by the telescopes.

Telescope mounts

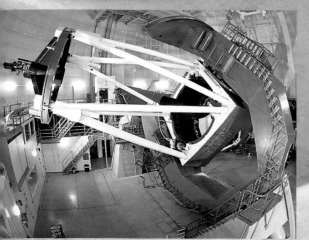

Telescopes are supported on stands called mounts. A blue-painted mount (left) holds the 11.5 ft. reflector at the Calar Alto Observatory in Spain. The mount not only takes the weight of the telescope, it also allows it to be positioned easily. At the push of a button the mount moves the telescope up and down and from side to side so it can point to anywhere in the sky. Automatic computer controls also keep the telescope tracked on an object, such as a star, as Earth turns. Otherwise the star would quickly move out of the telescope's view.

Observatory Earth

The world's most powerful telescopes are located on mountaintops around the world. Several telescopes occupy the same site, together forming an observatory. The telescopes work above the clouds, faraway from city lights where the air is clear, still, dry, and thin. Here astronomers look into the darkest skies above Earth and get the best view of the universe.

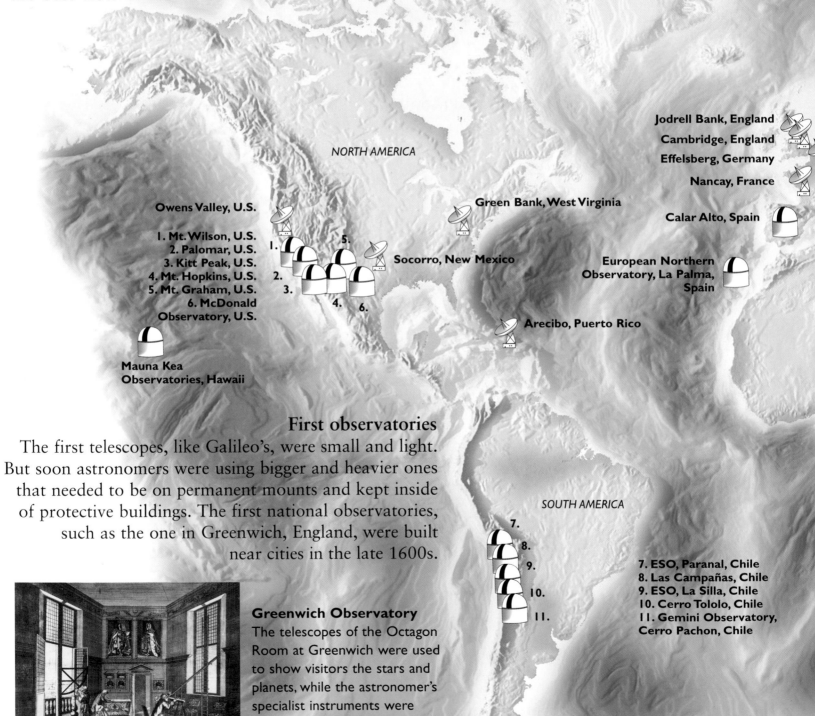

NORTH AMERICA

Owens Valley, U.S.

1. Mt. Wilson, U.S.
2. Palomar, U.S.
3. Kitt Peak, U.S.
4. Mt. Hopkins, U.S.
5. Mt. Graham, U.S.
6. McDonald Observatory, U.S.

Mauna Kea Observatories, Hawaii

Green Bank, West Virginia

Socorro, New Mexico

Arecibo, Puerto Rico

Jodrell Bank, England
Cambridge, England
Effelsberg, Germany
Nancay, France

Calar Alto, Spain

European Northern Observatory, La Palma, Spain

SOUTH AMERICA

7. ESO, Paranal, Chile
8. Las Campañas, Chile
9. ESO, La Silla, Chile
10. Cerro Tololo, Chile
11. Gemini Observatory, Cerro Pachon, Chile

First observatories

The first telescopes, like Galileo's, were small and light. But soon astronomers were using bigger and heavier ones that needed to be on permanent mounts and kept inside of protective buildings. The first national observatories, such as the one in Greenwich, England, were built near cities in the late 1600s.

Greenwich Observatory

The telescopes of the Octagon Room at Greenwich were used to show visitors the stars and planets, while the astronomer's specialist instruments were kept elsewhere.

Mountaintop observatories

In the late 1800s astronomers started to take advantage of the good observing conditions at remote mountaintop locations. The Lick Observatory in California, built in the 1880s, was the first permanent mountaintop observatory. Until the 1960s most observatories were in the Northern Hemisphere, and the southern skies were relatively unexplored. Today there are world-class, mountaintop observatories in the north and south.

Kitt Peak, Arizona
Kitt Peak National Observatory in Arizona dates from 1958. At first there were only two small telescopes. Today there are 15 major telescopes, each run by an American university or government institution.

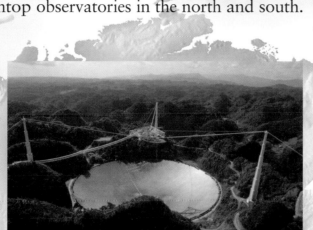

Arecibo radio telescope
The 1,000 ft. dish in Arecibo, Puerto Rico, is the largest single radio dish in the world. It is built in a natural hollow in the island's hills and faces different parts of the sky as it turns with Earth.

European Southern Observatory, Chile
In the 1960s a number of European countries joined together to build the European Southern Observatory in La Silla, Chile. Additional observatories are now located on neighboring mountain ridges.

Anglo-Australian Observatory
The Anglo-Australian Observatory is funded and run by the British and Australian governments. Astronomers from both countries have been viewing the southern sky from here for around 30 years.

ASIA

EUROPE

Mt. Pastukhov, Russia

AFRICA

Hartebeesthoek, South Africa

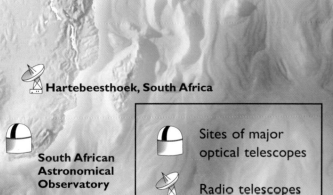

South African Astronomical Observatory

Sites of major optical telescopes

Radio telescopes

AUSTRALIA

12.
13.
14.

12. Narrabri, Australia
13. Anglo-Australian Observatory, Australia
14. Parkes, Australia

Invisible Universe

Our eyes let us see the stars in the sky. They collect light waves that travel across space and form these into images. Light is just one form of energy wave emitted by stars— there are others such as X-ray, infrared, and radio waves. If our eyes could collect the other kinds of rays, we would see so much more of the universe. Special telescopes, both on the ground and in space, allow astronomers to collect this extra information from the stars. Familiar objects are seen in a new way, and objects usually invisible are revealed. Although we have discovered more of the universe by collecting the range of wavelengths, astronomers think there is still much more to be found.

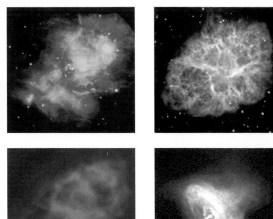

Filling in the picture
Astronomers have been collecting the different wavelengths from space for around 40 years. Each type of wavelength is collected and studied independently, and objects look very different in the various wavelengths. The Crab Nebula is the remains of a star that exploded in 1054. The infrared view is top left, the usual light wave view is top right, and underneath are the radio (above left), and X-ray view (above right).

The search for dark matter

Astronomers believe that everything we know about only makes up a tiny part of the material in the universe. As much as 95 percent of the universe is missing. If this material gave out light, radio, infrared, or other waves, we would detect it. It doesn't, but we know it's there because astronomers have seen the effects of its gravity and have identified places where some exists. They think the missing material, called dark matter, could be tiny particles smaller than atoms. One type of these particles is called WIMPs (weakly interactive massive particles). They haven't been found yet, but the search is on.

Dark matter map
The computer model above shows a part of the universe that is billions of light-years long. Dark matter (red) lies between the galaxies (blue). The dark matter's gravity bends the light (yellow) from the galaxies. If there was no dark matter, the light paths would be straight.

Collecting electromagnetic waves
Radio waves make it through Earth's atmosphere and are collected at sea level. Light also makes it through, but it is best collected at mountaintop sites, along with infrared waves. Other wavelengths do not get through and must be collected by telescopes in space.

Listening into space
Radio astronomy began in 1932 when Karl Jansky detected radio signals from the Milky Way. A radio dish telescope collects the radio waves. They are turned into electric signals and stored on computers for use by astronomers. The Very Large Array in New Mexico is made up of 27 dishes, each one 82 ft. across, working as a group.

Gamma rays

X-rays

Ultraviolet

Light

Infra-red

Radio

Energy spectrum
The full range of energy waves given off by objects in space is known as the electromagnetic spectrum. The various wavelengths reveal different aspects of the universe. Gamma rays have identified distant, exploding stars, and X rays have shown the location of black holes. Ultraviolet energy is given off by the hottest stars, infrared waves reveal newly born stars normally hidden by dust, and radio waves have provided evidence for the big bang theory.

Space explorers

Many astronomers would love to go into space and see for themselves what it is like. Although men traveled to the Moon between 1969–1972, and people now regularly spend time in space around Earth, we are not ready yet to go any farther. So astronomers stay on Earth and send spacecraft to explore and study the universe for them. Spacecraft do not need to eat or sleep or return home when their work is done. Astronomers use two types of craft—space probes and space telescopes.

Exploring Mars
Around 30 space probes have been sent to study Mars. *Pathfinder* landed on its surface in July 1997. It then opened up to release *Sojourner* (above), a buggy the size of a microwave oven, to drive over the Martian surface. *Sojourner* was operated by remote control from Earth.

Space robots

Space probes are robotic explorers sent into the solar system. In the last 40 years they have been sent to all of the planets in the solar system except Pluto. They have also visited moons, comets, and asteroids. A space probe is about the size of a car or minivan. It has its own power, computer and communication systems, cameras, and a set of experiments and instruments for investigating its target. Each probe is designed for a particular mission. It might fly by its target (such as a planet or moon), go into orbit around it, or land on it.

Launch into space
Space probes and satellites are launched into space by rockets. The *Ariane* rocket (left) launches European satellites and probes into space from its launch site at Kourou, French Guiana, South America.

Journey to Saturn

Even after a space probe is launched it can be years before it starts its work. The probe *Cassini* faced a seven-year journey after its launch to Saturn in October 1997. Its instruments were turned on while it flew by Jupiter, but the probe will only be fully operational once it reaches Saturn in 2004.

Investigating Titan

A small probe called *Huygens* (below) has hitched a ride onboard *Cassini*. It will investigate the atmosphere and surface of Titan, Saturn's largest moon.

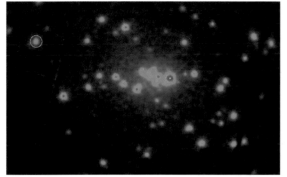

X-ray view

Astronomers hope that *XMM-Newton* will help them understand more about distant objects such as galaxies and black holes. This is an X-ray view of the central region of the Andromeda galaxy.

Eyes on the universe

Space telescopes are a type of satellite that look into space as they orbit Earth. Astronomers have been looking at the universe with space telescopes for around 40 years. They work in a similar way to Earth-based telescopes, by collecting and recording information from space objects. Some are working above us right now. Their advantage is that they are above Earth's atmosphere and weather. This means they can work 24 hours a day, 365 days a year, and they can collect wavelengths that do not travel through the atmosphere such as X rays.

XMM-Newton

The *XMM-Newton* space telescope has been collecting X rays since December 1999. The X rays are collected by sets of paper-thin mirrors placed within the telescope's three barrel-shaped entrances.

THE SOLAR SYSTEM

Earth belongs to a family of planets, moons, comets, and space rocks, all of which orbit the Sun. As a group these objects are called the solar system. They have been together for around 4.6 billion years, when they were made from a giant spinning cloud of gas and dust. The Sun was the first to form in the center of the cloud. Surrounding it was a spinning disk of leftover material, which over millions of years formed the nine planets. The Sun is the largest member of the solar system and has the strongest gravitational pull. The Sun's gravity keeps the group together.

Rock planets

Mercury, Venus, Earth, Mars, and Pluto are the rock planets. They began as tiny particles of dust and gas, which clumped together to form larger particles, then lumps, boulders, and finally giant spheres of rock—the planets.

Solar system model

In the past people learned about the solar system from models like this orrery (below). Its planets revolve around the central Sun.

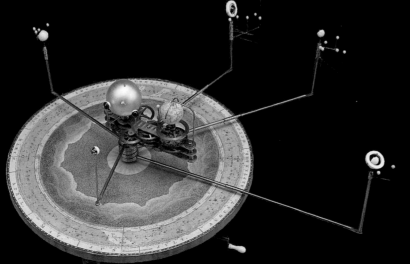

Mercury

Mercury is the closest planet to the Sun and spins around it the fastest.

Venus

Venus is the slowest spinning planet. It is also the hottest, with a thick atmosphere.

Earth

Earth has liquid water on its surface. Closer to the Sun water would boil, farther away it would freeze.

Observing the planets

Five planets—Mercury, Venus, Mars, Jupiter, and Saturn—are easy to see with the naked eye, if you know where to look! Planets are disk-shaped, unlike stars, which appear as pinpoints of bright light. Usually only one or two planets are visible in the same part of the sky. Occasionally more can be lined up in the sky, as shown here in the early evening in May 2002.

Saturn
Mars
Venus
Mercury

Distant gas giants

Jupiter, Saturn, Uranus, and Neptune do not have solid surfaces like the rock planets. What we can see is the top of a gas giant's atmosphere.

Moons and space rocks

Seven of the planets have moons—rocky bodies that orbit the planets like mini solar systems. There are at least 100 moons in our solar system. The largest is bigger than Mercury, and the smallest are hill-sized, potato-shaped lumps. Billions of space rocks, called asteroids, orbit the Sun between Mars and Jupiter. Farther away, closer to Neptune and Pluto, are icy space rocks—the Kuiper belt objects. Far beyond are trillions of comets that form the vast, spherical Oort Cloud.

Mars	**Jupiter**	**Saturn**	**Uranus**	**Neptune**	**Pluto**
Mars is around half the size of Earth and spins around once in about the same time, just over 24½ hours.	Jupiter is the largest and most massive planet and also the fastest spinner. It spins around in under 10 hours.	Saturn is the second-largest planet. It is almost 10 times as far away from the Sun as Earth.	Uranus' rings appear to go over its top rather than around its middle. This is because it is tilted on its side.	Neptune is the smallest, most distant of the gas giants. It is 30 times as far from the Sun as Earth.	Pluto is the most distant and smallest planet—smaller than Earth's moon. Its orbit takes almost 248 years.

The Sun

The Sun is a large ball of incredibly hot, bright gas.
It is one million mi. (1.4 million km) across—109 Earths
could fit across its face. It contains over 99 percent of all
material in the solar system. Like other stars, the Sun is not
a solid object, but we can detect a visible surface called the
photosphere. The temperature here is 9,932°F (5,500°C).
The Sun shines because it produces light energy. It has
been shining for around 4.6 billion years and will
continue to do so for the next five billion years or so.

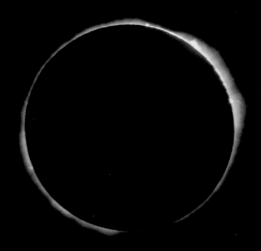

Sunspots and flares
The photosphere is a busy and violent place. Gas is
constantly swirling and shooting up from the surface
in jets, columns, and sheets. Dark spots,
hundreds or thousands of miles
wide, regularly appear,
and gigantic gas flares
arch over them.

The Sun's atmosphere
Beyond its bright and hectic
surface is the Sun's atmosphere,
stretching millions of miles into
space. The inner atmosphere,
the chromosphere (above),
and the outer one, the corona,
are not usually visible from
Earth. But during a total
solar eclipse the Sun's
atmosphere is revealed.

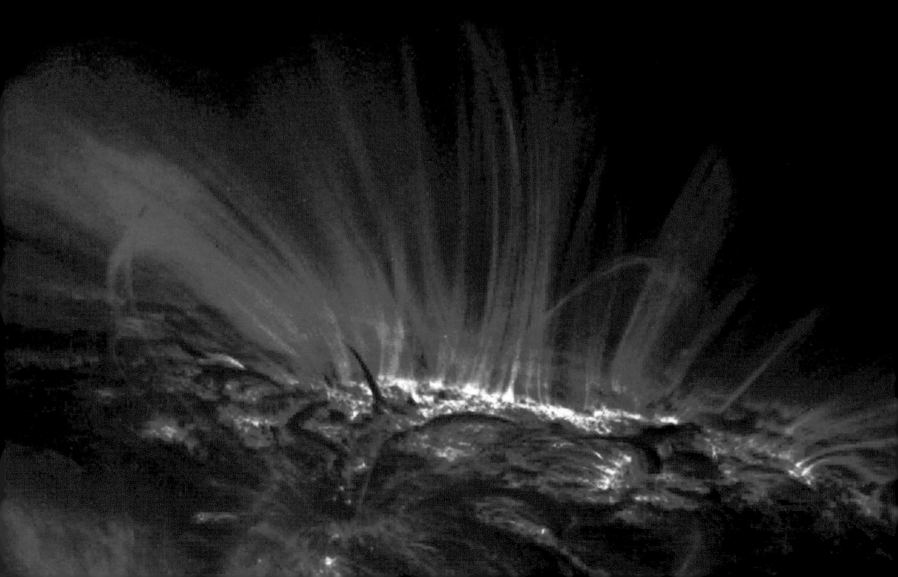

Inside the Sun

Around three fourths of the Sun is hydrogen. The rest is mostly helium with tiny amounts of other elements. Gravity keeps the gas together, pulling it toward the Sun's center and stopping it from drifting into space. In the center the gas is packed together and gets much hotter—around 60 percent of the Sun's gas is squashed into the core, where temperatures are an incredible 27 million°F (15 million°C). Here in the core hydrogen is converted into helium, producing huge amounts of energy. Every second around 0.6 billion tons of hydrogen is converted into helium. The energy slowly zigzags its way to the surface where it leaves the Sun, mostly as light and heat.

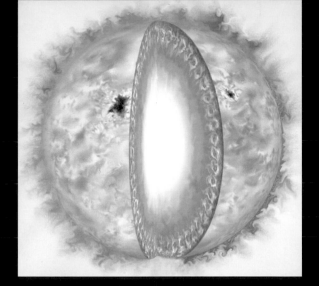

Light display

Occasionally, in areas near Earth's poles, skywatchers can view spectacular light shows. This is the aurora borealis, or northern lights, seen here above Alaska.

Discovering helium

Helium was discovered in the Sun before it was found on Earth. English astronomer Norman Lockyer was looking at a spectrum of the Sun's light in 1868. He saw a line across the spectrum, which could not have been made by any of the elements known on Earth. He realized it was made by a new element. He called it helium from the Greek word for sun, *helios*.

Looking at the Sun

The Sun is a familiar sight from Earth. But no one should look at the Sun directly. Its intense light can damage our eyes. Astronomers investigate the Sun by using special telescopes to record its details, which they study later. However, there are some solar displays we can watch such as an aurora, a show of colorful rays and streamers in the sky. This occurs when the solar wind, made up of incredibly tiny particles, spirals away from the Sun and travels far into space, journeying past the planets and out of the solar system. As the wind streams past Earth some of its particles enter our atmosphere and become trapped by magnetic lines around Earth's poles. They collide with air molecules that glow and create the aurora.

Earth: home planet

Earth is the biggest rock planet and the third one from the Sun. It is 7,909 mi. across. Every part of Earth is special to us, providing us with everything we need in order to survive. Anyone visiting Earth from another planet would see that our buildings, crops, and roads make their mark on Earth. The same visitor would also see a planet covered mostly by water with landmasses that change appearance by natural forces. They would experience temperatures from an icy -130°F (-90°C) to a searing 136°F (58°C), see dry, arid land and lush vegetation, and find life wherever they looked.

Eye on Earth
We still have a lot to learn about Earth. We investigate it from the ground and by using satellites from space. Satellites monitor such things as Earth's climate, its polar ice caps, the growth of crops, and ocean currents.

Life
Earth is the only planet where life is known to exist. It is found all around the globe—on every continent, in its oceans, and flying through its air.

Each 23.9-hour turn of Earth brings night and day, and every 365.25-day year, as Earth orbits the Sun, brings the seasons.

Water cycle
Water moves constantly between the planet and its atmosphere. In this rain forest rain has fallen, and mist is rising. It will condense into clouds, and rain will fall once more.

Explosive Earth
Earth's outer shell is broken up into pieces called plates. These move against and away from each other, causing earthquakes and volcanic eruptions such as that of Mount Etna in Sicily.

Changing face
Some changes to Earth are immediate and others happen slowly. Both air and water can slowly erode Earth's surface. Wind has sculpted rocks in the Utah Desert, and the Greenland ice sheet erodes land as it moves.

Blue planet

From space it is easy to see that water covers most of Earth's surface—a total of 71 percent. Water gives our planet its distinctive color. Also visible is some of the atmosphere that surrounds Earth. This is the thin layer of gas, rich in nitrogen, that protects Earth from harmful energy waves, maintains a safe temperature range, and provides the air we breathe. In the 1860s English scientist James Glaisher made 28 daring balloon ascents to study the atmosphere. He and his companion flew to altitudes of around six miles (10km), where the atmosphere is so thin they almost lost their lives.

Earth's land
Africa is visible here below Earth's clouds. It is one of the planet's seven landmasses, or continents.

Earth's Moon

The Moon is our closest neighbor in space. It orbits around us at a distance of 238,390 mi. and journeys with Earth as it makes its yearly orbit around the Sun. It is a cold, lifeless ball of rock around one fourth the size of Earth. It has no atmosphere or liquid water, and its dusty surface is covered with hollows called craters. The Moon is by far the largest object in the night sky, and it shines brightly by reflected sunlight. It has been studied by astronomers for thousands of years and is the only place outside of Earth that humans have visited.

The same face

Only one side of the Moon is ever visible from Earth. It is called the nearside. This is because the Moon spins around once in the same amount of time that it takes to orbit once around Earth. See how the same side (marked by a dot) always faces Earth but spins and orbits in a 27.3-day period.

The Moon's phases

The Moon seems to change its shape gradually from day to day. It is not really changing. The nearside of the Moon is always facing us, but we only see the part lit up by the Sun. When the Moon's nearside is unlit, it is virtually invisible. This is called a new moon. When the nearside is fully lit, it is called a full moon. Each different shape is a phase of the Moon. One complete cycle, from new moon to new moon, takes 29.5 days.

Formation of the Moon

Most astronomers think the Moon was formed when a Mars-sized space rock collided into young Earth around 4.5 billion years ago. Molten rock from the two bodies splashed into space. This made a ring around Earth. Eventually the material clumped together to form the Moon. The Moon then cooled, its rock solidified, and a surface crust formed.

Surface features

We can see features on the Moon's surface using only our eyes. The dark patches are *maria*—areas of volcanic lava—and the light areas are older, higher land.

Man on the Moon

Between 1969 and 1972, 26 American astronauts traveled to the Moon. Twelve of them walked on its surface and explored six different sites. They brought back 2,000 samples of rocks and dust to Earth.

Studying the Moon

The Moon has been studied in more detail than any other space object. Astronomers have used their eyes and telescopes on Earth and in space to study it, and more than 60 spacecrafts have successfully traveled to the Moon. We know what the Moon is like today and what it was like in the past. Around four billion years ago it was bombarded by space rocks, which formed craters and pushed up mountains. Three billion years ago lava seeped from inside the Moon and flooded some craters, forming the *maria*. For the last two billion years the Moon has hardly changed.

Rock worlds

Mercury and Pluto are the two smallest planets in the solar system. Pluto is tiny, only 1,407 mi. (2,270km) across, and Mercury is 3,026 mi. (4,880km)—one smaller and one bigger than Earth's Moon. Each is a sphere of rock, but they are opposites in almost every way. Mercury is the closest planet to the Sun and gets incredibly hot. It is the fastest orbiter of all the planets, traveling around the Sun once every 88 days. Pluto is the most distant planet— 100 times farther from the Sun than Mercury—and is a desolate, frozen world. It is the slowest orbiter and takes almost 248 years to travel around the Sun. Both planets are difficult to see from Earth and are largely unknown.

Seeing Mercury

Mercury is hard to observe because it is never far from the Sun in our sky. In the 1920s French astronomer Eugène Antoniadi drew maps of markings he observed on its surface. In 1974 we saw what Mercury is really like when the first pictures were transmitted to Earth by *Mariner 10*.

Hot and cold

It is scorching hot on the part of Mercury that faces the Sun—around 842°F (450°C), much hotter than a kitchen oven. But the temperature drops to a freezing cold -292°F (-180°C) at night because Mercury has such a thin atmosphere, much too thin to keep in the heat.

Mercury—cratered world

Mercury is a dry, cratered, dead world whose surface has barely changed in millions of years. Its craters were formed when the young planet was bombarded by space rocks, and its plains were formed when lava flooded onto the surface. Only one space probe, *Mariner 10*, has visited Mercury so far. It flew by the planet three times in 1974–1975. Astronomers are now ready to return. The U.S. *Messenger* probe will be there in 2008–2009, and a European probe called *BepiColombo* will be launched a year or so later.

Pluto from Earth

Pluto was discovered in 1930, and its one moon, Charon, which is around half of Pluto's size, was discovered in 1978. Even the powerful Hubble Space Telescope cannot give us detailed views of these worlds. Looking at Pluto is like trying to look at a golf ball 60 mi. away.

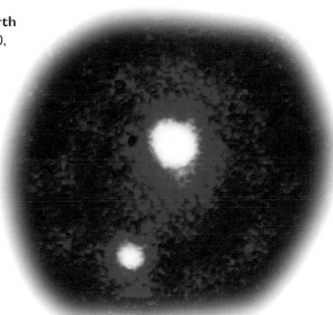

Discovery

American astronomer Clyde Tombaugh discovered Pluto from the Lowell Observatory in Flagstaff, Arizona. Night after night he took photographs of the starry sky. Pluto appeared as a dot that changed position from image to image compared with stars, which are stationary.

Pluto—odd planet out

Remote Pluto is the planet we know the least about. Its distance and size make it difficult to observe, and it is the only planet not yet explored by space probes. Astronomers hope to change this and are planning to send a mission to Pluto by 2020. From Earth we can tell Pluto is very different to its neighbors. Its size, structure, and composition are nothing like those of the gas giants. It also has a strange orbit, which is the least circular of all the planets' orbits and has the biggest tilt. These differences make some astronomers think that Pluto is not a planet but a large, icy object belonging to the Kuiper Belt.

Pluto's path

Pluto's strange orbit is shown above in green. For about 20 years of each orbit Pluto is within Neptune's orbit and is closer to the Sun than to Neptune.

Distant worlds

In this artist's impression we see Pluto in the sky above Charon. In the distance is the Sun. Pluto is too far from the Sun to receive any obvious light or heat. Its temperature is around -364°F, and its surface is permanently frozen.

Near neighbors

Venus and Mars are Earth's closest planetary neighbors.
All three are spheres of rock, but they are very different
on the surface. The atmosphere on Venus, which is closer
to the Sun than Earth, is hot and suffocating. The temperature
can reach an incredible 867°F (464°C), over eight times hotter
than the highest temperature recorded on Earth. Mars is farther
away from the Sun and is cold and barren. The temperature at its
poles is an icy -248°F (-120°C). Both Venus and Mars are easy to
see in Earth's sky, and they've been observed by astronomers for
thousands of years. But we've only known what they are really
like since spacecraft were able
to take a closer look.

Slow spinner
Venus spins slower
than any of the other
planets—once every
243 days. This is longer
than the time it takes to
orbit the Sun. Its clouds spin
around the planet much faster. They
are mainly made up of carbon dioxide,
and they trap the Sun's heat, helping
make Venus such a hot place.

View from Earth
Venus is easy to spot
from Earth, but its thick,
cloudy atmosphere stops us from
observing its surface. It also stops
most of the sunlight that shines on
Venus from reaching the ground,
making it a very gloomy place.

Volcanic surface
Astronomers had their first good look under Venus' clouds in 1975
when a space probe survived its journey through the atmosphere and
sent back an image of a rocky surface. More recently astronomers have
used radar to see through the clouds to the surface below. In the early
1990s *Magellan* (above) used radar to map almost all of Venus'
surface. It showed a rocky landscape formed by volcanic activity.
There are huge volcanoes and lava flows all over Venus. Over 150
volcanoes are more than 62 mi. wide. Maat Mons (left) is one
of the biggest. It measures 124 mi. across and 5 mi. high.

Investigating Mars

Mars has always fascinated people. It is a rock planet like our own and, after Earth, is the planet most likely to support life. Books and films have described imaginary creatures, called Martians, living on Mars and even invading Earth. Astronomers have been sending space probes to Mars over the past 40 years in order to find out what the planet is really like. Many probes have orbited the planet, others have landed on it, and a small remote-controlled vehicle has driven across its surface. They've made detailed maps of the planet, studied its weather, and tested its rocks for signs of life.

Studying Mars
Percival Lowell studied Mars from his observatory in Arizona in the 1890s. He mistakenly believed he could see canals on the surface that he believed had been dug by an intelligent life-form living on Mars.

A day on Mars
Mars is around half the size of Earth and one-and-a-half times farther from the Sun. It spins around once in just over 24½ hours, making its day length very similar to Earth's.

The red planet
Mars has a very thin atmosphere, so we can usually look directly at its reddish surface. It is called the "red planet" because it appears red in Earth's sky. Its color comes from iron oxide (rust) in the planet's soil.

Rocky landscape
The surface of Mars is like a huge, frozen, rocky desert dotted with volcanoes much larger than anything on Earth. Olympus Mons (left), the largest volcano in the solar system, stands 15 mi. high and 372 mi. across. A vast canyon system, the Valles Marineris (below), measuring 2790 mi. from end to end and 5 mi. deep, cuts across the planet.

Space rocks

There are billions of lumps of rock in the solar system—these are called asteroids. More than 90 percent of them are found in a doughnut-shaped ring between the orbits of Mars and Jupiter. Astronomers have known about the asteroids here, in the Main Belt, ever since they discovered Ceres in 1801. They now know about a second belt of icy space rocks—the Kuiper Belt—at the edge of the planetary solar system. The first of these was discovered in September 1992. Astronomers study asteroids in space and others down on Earth.

Eros
Eros has been studied in greater detail than any other asteroid. The space probe *NEAR* took images of Eros from different angles before landing on it in February 2001. The images are colored to help scientists study Eros's surface and structure.

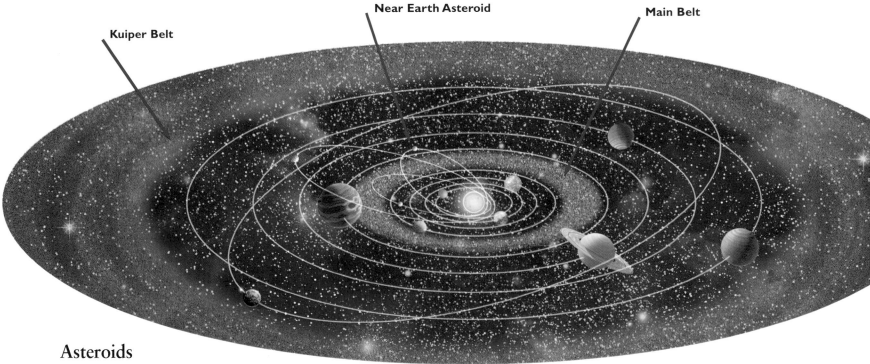

Kuiper Belt

Near Earth Asteroid

Main Belt

Asteroids

Asteroids are rocky material that was left over when the planets and moons were formed 4.6 billion years ago. They come in a range of sizes—from boulder- and mountain-sized to the biggest, Ceres, at 578 mi. across. All but the largest are irregular in shape, like potatoes. Each one takes just a few years to orbit around the Sun and spins as it travels, turning only once in hours or weeks. Some asteroids are not in the Main Belt but instead follow orbits that bring them close to Earth's orbit. These are the Near Earth Asteroids—Eros is one.

Ida and Gaspra
Ida (right) has a tiny moon of its own called Dactyl. Gaspra (far right) measures 7 mi. across and is found near the inner edge of the Main Belt.

Impact with Earth

On every continent on Earth there is evidence that asteroids have collided into our planet. An asteroid crashing into Earth produces a crater. The size of the crater depends on the size of the colliding rock. There are around 160 craters on Earth. Most of these were formed more than 100 million years ago. The Wolfe Creek Crater in Australia (left) is 2,854 ft. across and was formed around 300,000 years ago.

Chicxulub

The Chicxulub Crater was formed around 65 million years ago when a mountain-sized space rock struck Earth. Material sent up into the atmosphere blocked the Sun's heat and light for months, and most life, including the dinosaurs, died.

Down to Earth

Space rocks that land on Earth are called meteorites. Around 3,000 of them weighing more than 2.21 lbs. each land every year. Most fall into the sea, but the rest hit land. Scientists hunt for meteorites in the undisturbed and barren regions of Earth. Most of the thousands of meteorites that have been found are pieces of asteroids. But more than 20 have arrived here from the Moon and more than 20 more from Mars.

Meteorite hunt

Antarctica is a great place to hunt for meteorites. The dark rocks are easy to see on the ice (below). Once collected thin slices of the meteorite can be studied closely (left).

The king

Jupiter is a huge planet—the biggest in the solar system. It has the largest family of moons and is the fastest spinner, turning around once in less than ten hours. Jupiter is a freezing cold -116°F at its surface but an amazing 54,032°F in its core. It was the first of the giant planets to be visited by spacecrafts when *Pioneer 10* flew by it in 1973. Since then the two *Voyagers* and the *Galileo* probe have investigated the planet.

Great Red Spot
The main feature of Jupiter's surface is the Great Red Spot, an enormous hurricane more than twice the size of Earth. Astronomers have been watching this storm change appearance for more than 300 years.

Inside Jupiter

Jupiter is mostly made up of hydrogen—the element that stars are made from—with some helium. If Jupiter had been made of around 50 times more hydrogen, it would have turned into a star. Jupiter does not have a solid surface but instead has a 620-mi.-deep shell of hydrogen and helium gas as its atmosphere. Below this outer layer is liquid hydrogen and helium. Deep inside is a solid core.

Even bigger
Jupiter currently measures 88,650 mi. from side to side. It was much bigger than this when it was young. The planet has been shrinking for millions of years and contracts by around one inch each year.

Stormy weather

When we look at Jupiter, we are looking at the top layer of its atmosphere. This is made up of different colored bands. The bright ones—called zones— are rising gas. The darker ones—called belts—are falling gas. Jupiter's rapid spin, combined with the rising heat from inside the planet, create atmospheric turbulence, very fast winds, and raging storms.

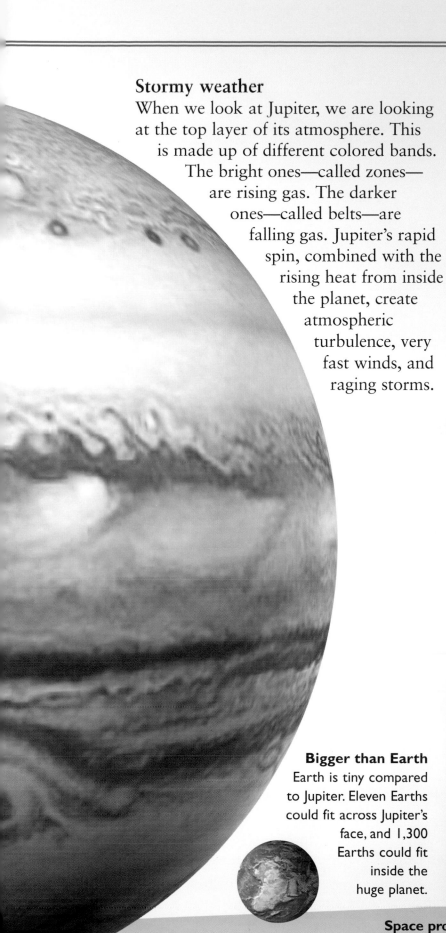

King of the planets

When early astronomers named Jupiter, they did not know that it was the largest planet. But they must have seen that it was one of the brightest objects in the sky. They named it after the king of the Roman gods.

View from Earth

Jupiter is hundreds of millions of miles from Earth, but it is easy to spot in our sky. It reflects the Sun's light well and looks like a bright silver star to our eyes. The bands across its surface and the four largest of its moons can be seen through a small telescope.

Bigger than Earth

Earth is tiny compared to Jupiter. Eleven Earths could fit across Jupiter's face, and 1,300 Earths could fit inside the huge planet.

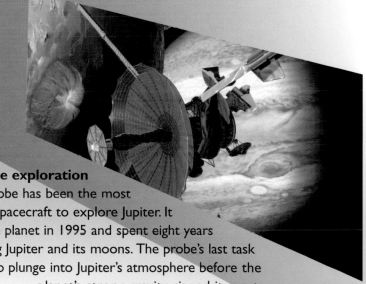

Space probe exploration

The *Galileo* probe has been the most successful spacecraft to explore Jupiter. It arrived at the planet in 1995 and spent eight years investigating Jupiter and its moons. The probe's last task was to plunge into Jupiter's atmosphere before the planet's strong gravity ripped it apart.

Jupiter

Saturn

Ringed worlds

The four largest planets in the solar system—
Jupiter, Saturn, Uranus, and Neptune—have a lot
in common. They are all distant, cold, and colorful
worlds whose outer surfaces are made up of gas,
and all have rings around them. They are all mostly
made up of hydrogen, but other elements in their
outer layers give them their distinctive colors. The
rings of all four planets look solid from a distance.
But when seen close-up, it is clear they are made up
of billions of individual pieces of rocks that orbit
around their parent planet like tiny moons.

Clear view
Dutch astronomer Christiaan
Huygens observed Saturn and
worked out that the planet
had a ring of material around
it. He published his
theory in 1655.

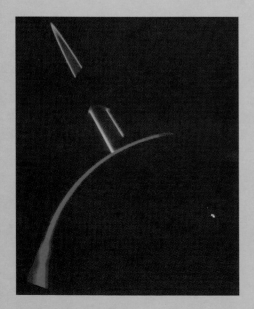

Jupiter's ring
Jupiter's faint ring
system was discovered
by the *Voyager I* space
probe in 1979. It is
made up of a handful
of rings formed from
dust pieces. The dust
was knocked off the
planet's inner moons
in Jupiter's past.

Lord of the rings
When Galileo looked at Saturn in 1610, he spotted
something on both sides of the planet. Saturn seemed
to have "ears." Galileo thought these must be moons.
But during the 1650s Christiaan Huygens observed
Saturn when the planet was farther along its orbit.
He was able to make out a ring surrounding the
planet. Both Galileo and Huygens had seen Saturn's
main rings (illustrated top). In fact, Saturn has many
more rings than this. There are very faint rings
stretching four times as far from the planet
as the main ring system.

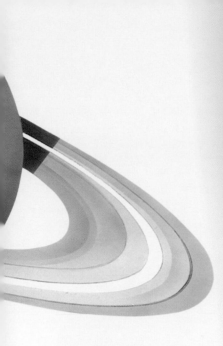

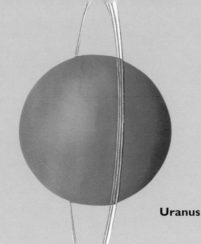

Uranus

Neptune

Changing view

As Saturn moves around the Sun on its orbit we see its rings from different angles. Twice during each orbit the edges of the rings are facing us and are almost impossible to see. For the remainder of the time we see a varying amount of them, from either above or below.

Changing Neptune

A giant cloud system, the Great Dark Spot, was discovered on Neptune's surface by *Voyager 2* in 1989. But it had disappeared by the time the Hubble Space Telescope was pointed at Neptune only five years later.

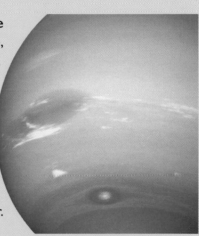

Discovering Uranus and Neptune

Until 1781 astronomers believed Saturn was the most distant planet. In that year English astronomer William Herschel discovered Uranus, which is over twice as far from the Sun as Saturn. Its ring system was discovered in 1977. Neptune was discovered by German astronomer Johann Galle in 1846. Much of our knowledge of these two distant planets came from the only probe that has visited them. This was *Voyager 2* in the 1980s. It provided close-up views and discovered Neptune's ring and moons around both of the planets.

Rings in close-up

Saturn has a complex ring system. The rings are made up of hundreds of ringlets. Each ringlet is made out of chunks of icy rocks and dust and follows individual orbits around Saturn. The main rings are made up of chunks the size of a house; the fainter rings are made up of smaller, pebble-sized ones.

Uranus and family

It is difficult to observe Uranus because it is so far from us. Today's large, Earth-based telescopes, however, reveal its ring system and larger moons. From left to right the moons pictured here are: Titania, Umbriel, Miranda, Ariel, and Oberon.

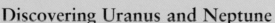

Planetary moons

There are more than 100 moons in the solar system. Between them they orbit around seven of the planets—only Mercury and Venus do not have moons. The smallest moons are the size of a small town, and the largest are bigger than the smallest planets. Until 30 years ago we knew about only 33 moons, but more were discovered when the two *Voyager* space probes flew by the ringed planets in the 1980s. Since then more powerful telescopes and improved techniques mean that we have been able to discover more and more.

Origins
Jupiter has the largest family of moons. More than 50 have been identified, and astronomers are looking for more. The larger moons, such as Ganymede, were formed when Jupiter was made. Its smaller moons are asteroids captured by Jupiter's gravity. Mars has two asteroid moons—Phobos and Deimos.

Saturn's moons
Astronomers have identified 30 moons orbiting Saturn—and there are probably more. Like most other moons in the solar system, they are named after figures from ancient mythology. Tethys (above right) and Dione (above left) are named after two sisters of the god Saturn.

Ganymede and Janus
Jupiter's Ganymede (left) is the largest of all of the moons in the solar system. It is 3,262 mi. wide—bigger than both Mercury and Pluto. Saturn's Janus, at 118 mi. across, is a small moon. Even smaller ones, 1–3 mi. across, are known.

Discovering moons

The first moons to be discovered—apart from Earth's Moon—were found around Jupiter and Saturn in the 1600s. Italian-French astronomer Giovanni Cassini (left) made a study of Saturn and discovered Iapetus, Rhea, Tethys, and Dione, as well as the gap in Saturn's ring that is named after him. The first of Uranus's 21 moons was discovered in 1787, and Triton, the largest of Neptune's eight moons, was discovered in 1846. Pluto's only moon, Charon, was detected in 1978.

Closer investigation

Space probes have shown us what many of the moons are like. Each one is a rock or rock and ice body. The small, irregular-shaped ones look very similar. But the large, round ones have vastly different features. There are ice volcanoes, frozen oceans, sulfur spurts, red-hot lava, and grooved and cratered surfaces. The *Cassini* probe will reveal more about Saturn's moons, particularly Titan (left), which is the only moon with a substantial atmosphere. Its surface is beneath thick, moving orange clouds.

Io and Europa

Io and Europa, two of Jupiter's larger moons, are contrasting worlds. Io (below left) is covered in volcanoes, molten rocks, and sulfur lakes. Gas eruptions and flowing lava happen constantly. Europa's surface (below right) is icy and smooth. Underneath the ice is a liquid ocean, which might be the home of some form of life.

Ice kingdoms

There are around ten trillion comets in the solar system. Each one is a mountain-sized world of snow, ice, and dust—a giant cosmic snowball. Together they make an enormous sphere called the Oort Cloud, which surrounds the planetary part of the solar system. The cloud's closest edge is around 372 billion mi. away, and its farthest edge is around four trillion mi. from us. Even the closest comets are too small and distant to be seen. It is only when a comet leaves the cloud and travels in toward the Sun that we can see it.

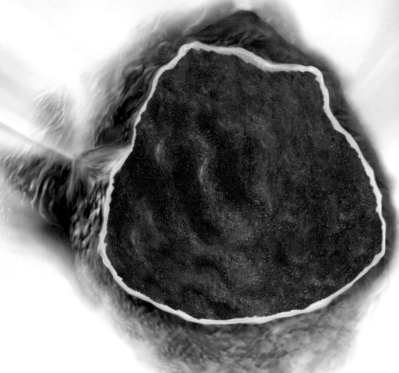

Halley's nucleus
We have seen the nucleui of only two comets. The first was that of Halley's Comet (left). The space probe *Giotto* flew to within 372 mi. of the 10-mi.-long snowball nucleus in March 1986.

Cosmic snowball
Comets are often described as dirty snowballs because they are lumps of snow and rocky dust. They are not, in fact, ball-shaped but are irregular in shape—more like a potato or a peanut. A slice through one would show that a layer of dust covers the snowy interior.

Fear of comets
For centuries the sudden appearance of a comet in the sky was thought to be a sign of a coming disaster. Montezuma II, the last emperor of the Aztec people, took the arrival of this comet (below) and another brilliant comet as an omen that he would lose his empire. In 1519 he did.

Understanding comets
The first step to understanding comets came in 1705 when English astronomer Edmond Halley showed that a comet can return again and again to Earth's sky. In 1951 American astronomer Fred Whipple proposed the idea that a cometary nucleus is like a dirty snowball. He was proved right when *Giotto* investigated Halley's Comet in 1986. Astronomers will soon be able to add to their knowledge of comets when the *Stardust* space probe returns a sample from a comet and *Rosetta* lands on one in around ten years.

In Earth's sky

Once in a while a comet leaves the Oort Cloud and follows a path into the inner solar system. When the comet is closer to the Sun than to Mars, the Sun's warmth turns its snow into gas. This forms a large head, called a coma, around the nucleus. Gas and dust are swept away from the nucleus and form tails. The comet is now large enough and bright enough to be seen from Earth. Around 750 such comets have been seen so far. The blue gas tail and whiter dust tail of Comet Hale-Bopp (right) were clearly visible as it traveled across our sky in 1997.

Returning comets

Around 150 comets follow orbits that return them to our skies in a period of less than 200 years. A new coma and tails develop each time one travels close to the Sun. They then shrink after a few months as the comet moves away. The coma can be 62,000 mi. across, and the tails can be 62 million mi. long.

Shooting stars

The dust lost by a comet as it travels close to the Sun is scattered along the comet's orbital path. It forms a meteoroid stream—a ring of tiny dust particles no bigger than grains of sand. As Earth travels around the Sun it passes through around 20 meteoroid streams each year. When a meteoroid enters Earth's atmosphere, it heats up and produces a trail of light in our sky—a meteor. Meteors are commonly called shooting stars because that is how they appear in our sky.

Shower of light

The Leonid Meteor Shower is seen in November each year as Earth passes through the dust stream of Comet Tempel-Tuttle. This image was made on November 17, 1966 when a record rate of 60,000 meteors per hour was recorded.

THE REALM OF THE STARS

The universe is full of stars. There are billions and billions of them—more than any other type of space object. Each one is a huge sphere of incredibly hot, luminous gas. A star's gravity holds the gas together. The stars differ in brightness, color, size, age, and mass. Astronomers are especially interested in mass, which is the amount of gas that makes up a star. Some stars are much less massive than the Sun, while others are many times more massive. Mass establishes a star's other characteristics and determines its future.

Understanding stars
English astronomer Arthur Eddington (above right) was fascinated by stars and spent a lot of his life studying how they work. In particular he showed that a star's heat and light energy are produced by changes inside of the star. He is seen here in 1933 with the scientist Albert Einstein.

Galaxies

Stars are not scattered randomly through space but instead exist in galaxies. Each one is made up of billions of stars, and there are vast distances between them. Our local star, the Sun, is in the Milky Way galaxy. The Andromeda galaxy (right) is one of the galaxies closest to ours.

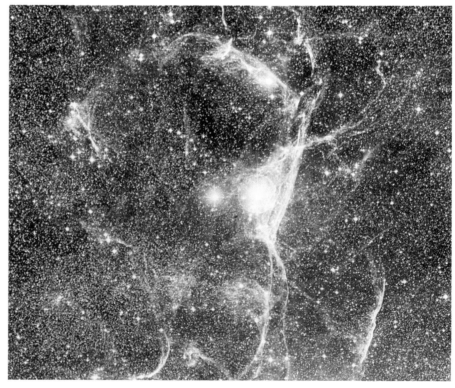

Stellar life cycle

Stars are being created all the time inside of galaxies. They are formed within giant clouds of gas and dust, and hundreds or thousands of stars are created together in a cluster. The stars in some clusters drift apart slowly, while those in other clusters stay packed together until they die. The most massive stars have the shortest lives, living for only a few million years. Less massive stars, such as the Sun, live a lot longer—for billions of years. The material of dying stars is expelled back into space. It eventually becomes part of a cloud of gas and dust, and this is used to create new stars.

Star brightness

From Earth we see that stars differ in brightness. But this is not a true picture because the stars are at varied distances from us. A star might appear bright just because it is close. Astronomers are interested in both the apparent brightness of stars and the real brightness. Real brightness is the luminosity—the amount of light a star produces.

Stellar recycling

Almost 12,000 years ago a star exploded and blasted its material into space. This formed the ribbons and sheets of gas and dust we call the Vela supernova remnant. In millions or billions of years the material will be used to form new stars.

Seeing stars

There are thousands of stars in the sky that can be seen using just our eyes. In cities only the brightest can be seen, but in areas where there are no street or house lights the sky can be very dark. Here, on a clear, moonless night, the sky is full of stars. Imaginary patterns, called constellations, drawn around the brighter stars help stargazers recognize individual stars and locate objects in the sky. Many show people and creatures from old myths and stories. The first were devised around 4,000 years ago by the Greeks and Babylonians. Eventually Islamic and then European peoples adopted these constellations. Today Earth's sky is divided into 88 constellations used by stargazers around the world.

Perseus
This Arabic constellation picture shows the Greek hero Perseus. The star Algol marks the demon's head.

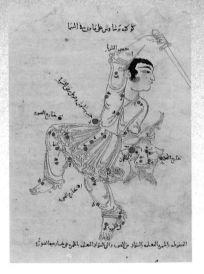

Changing skies
What stars you see in the sky depends on where you are on Earth, the time of year, and the time of night. These stargazers are looking up at Gemini, the twins (top left), Orion, the hunter (top center), and Taurus, the bull (top right). They are looking at the constellations in the Northern Hemisphere sky on a February night.

Bright stars

Many of the night sky's bright stars have names. The brightest of all is Sirius in the constellation Canis Major, the great dog. Its name comes from the Greek word for "scorching." Other names, such as Algol in the constellation Perseus, are Arabic in origin. Algol comes from the Arabic word for "demon's head." In Greek mythology Perseus cut off the head of the gorgon Medusa, and he is shown holding it in his hand.

Scorpius

Scorpius, the scorpion, is a zodiac constellation and one of the first to be devised. In Greek mythology this is the scorpion that used its sting to kill Orion. It can be seen from the Southern Hemisphere and from the lower latitudes of the Northern Hemisphere.

Hercules

Hercules is the fifth-largest constellation, visible from all but the most southerly of Earth's land. Hercules was the Greek hero who completed 12 tasks. One was to kill a dragon, and Hercules is shown with his foot on the head of the dragon—the constellation Draco.

Phoenix

Many of the constellations in the southern sky were devised only after navigators and explorers sailed south. Phoenix was one of 12 invented by two Dutch navigators at the end of the 1500s. This constellation is best seen from the Southern Hemisphere.

Crux

Crux, the Southern Cross, is the smallest constellation in the sky but is easy to see. Its stars were once part of Centaurus, the centaur, and were only formed into Crux in the late 1500s. Southern Hemisphere stargazers will find Crux in the Milky Way.

Giants and dwarfs

Stars fall into different types. The name of each type, such as red dwarf and blue giant, tells us about the color, temperature, and size of the star. The giants are tens of times the size of the Sun. Even larger are the supergiants, which can be up to a thousand times bigger than the Sun. Stars such as the Sun are called main-sequence stars, and these are all dwarfs. Other types of dwarfs are tiny in comparison.

Brown dwarf
New stars are forming in the pillars of gas and dust of the Eagle Nebula. Those formed of too little mass never produce light and heat. These are the brown dwarfs.

Star types
Early in the 1900s astronomers were studying the connection between stars' characteristics. Two astronomers working independently, Danish Ejnar Hertzsprung (above left) and American Henry Russell (above right), realized that stars fall into different types—giants and dwarfs depending on their temperature and luminosity.

White dwarf

A white dwarf is a dying star. It has run out of gas to convert and will soon stop producing light and heat. All that is left for it to do now is to slowly cool and shrink. Its material gets more and more densely packed as it shrinks to around the size of Earth.

Changing stars

Most stars are made up of mainly hydrogen and helium gas. Deep inside a star the hydrogen is converted into helium in a process called nuclear fusion. Energy, such as heat and light, is produced in the process. In some stars the helium is then converted into other elements such as oxygen and carbon. A star changes its size and color as it uses up one gas and moves on to convert another. This means that a star can be both a giant and a dwarf in its lifetime, as well as move through a range of colors.

Red supergiant

Betelgeuse, in the constellation of Orion, is a red supergiant star. All stars are incredibly hot, but a red star is one of the coolest. It is only around 5,432°F. The Sun and other yellow stars are hotter—around 9,932°F. Blue stars, which are the hottest of all, are around 54,032°F.

The Sun's future

Eventually the Sun will become a planetary nebula (5). It will start to die as it sheds material from its outer layers. The remaining material will squeeze together to make a star around the size of Earth—a white dwarf (6).

The Sun today

The Sun is now halfway through its time as a main-sequence star (3). It will stay like this for around five billion years more. As its hydrogen is used up the Sun will expand, and its surface will cool and turn red. It will be a red giant, up to 100 times bigger (4).

The Sun's beginnings

The Sun, like other stars, was created inside of a large cloud of gas and dust. It formed from cloud material collecting together (1). The material in the young Sun's center was hot and tightly packed. When it reached 18 million °F, nuclear fusion started. Energy was produced, and the Sun started to shine (2).

Explosive finish

Stars can take billions of years to die or can end their lives suddenly. The way that each star dies is not by chance. Its end has been certain since the start of its life. A star's death, like the course of its life, is determined by its mass—the amount of material it is made up of. Stars with much more mass than the Sun end their lives in a spectacular explosion, suddenly blowing themselves apart. Stars made up of less material have a slow but colorful death.

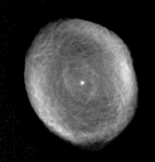

The Spirograph
All planetary nebulae have identification numbers. Some also have unofficial names. The Spirograph took its name from the drawing instrument and the patterns it creates.

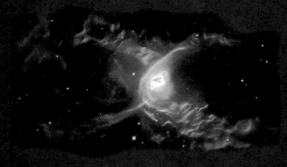

The Red Spider
620 mps winds blast out from the white dwarf in the center of this planetary nebula. The surrounding gas and dust glow brightly and form a spider shape.

Bursts of color

Stars made of less than around eight times the mass of the Sun die slowly. The process starts when they shed their outer layers of gas and transform into a colorful star called a planetary nebula. They will be like this for tens of thousands of years until the material finally disperses into space. At the heart of the nebula is a white dwarf, the remains of the original star, which will cool and die over billions of years.

The Butterfly
Jets of gas burst from the heart of this planetary nebula to form butterfly wings. There are two stars in the center. One is a white dwarf, the remains of the red giant that pushed its outer layers into space around 1,200 years ago.

Eta Carinae is one of the most massive
stars known—about 100 times more
massive than the Sun. It had an explosive
outburst in 1843 and was briefly the
second brightest star in our sky. It is
expected to die in one final explosion.

The Cat's Eye

Today's powerful telescopes
show the central star and
glowing material of nebulae
such as the Cat's Eye. But
when the first of these stars
were discovered 200 years
ago, the telescopes showed
them as planetlike disks. So
they were given the name
planetary nebulae.

Exploding stars

Stars with more than
around eight times the
Sun's mass blow themselves
apart. The exploding star is
called a supernova and looks
like a bright, new star. A core
of star material is left behind.
The future of this core depends
on its mass. A star three times
the mass of the Sun produces
a black hole. One with less
makes a tiny, very dense
neutron star—around the
size of a large city.

Discovery of pulsars

The Crab Nebula is the remains of a supernova
that exploded almost 1,000 years ago. In its center
is a neutron star. The star spins around 30 times
per second. The first spinning neutron star, called
a pulsar, was discovered in 1967 when British
astronomer Jocelyn Bell Burnell recorded
radio waves from the star as it turned.

Black hole

A black hole is produced as the core
of a star collapses in on itself. Its gravity
is so strong that anything falling onto it is
trapped forever. Even light cannot escape
from it, and so the hole will appear black.

Islands in the universe

There are billions of galaxies in the universe. Each one is a vast group of stars held together by its own gravity. A single galaxy contains billions or trillions of stars and clouds of gas and dust. Galaxies are very large and exist at huge distances apart, like distant islands scattered through space. As we look out from our galaxy, the Milky Way (right), we can see a few galaxies using only our eyes—these appear to be smudges of light. Powerful telescopes are used to reveal other galaxies and their details.

Breakthrough
In the 1920s American astronomer Edwin Hubble showed that there are other galaxies besides our own, that they conform to a set of basic shapes, and that galaxies are always moving apart.

Galaxy types

Galaxies are grouped according to their shape. A spiral is disk-shaped with a bright central bulge and spiraling arms of stars. In a barred spiral the center is bar-shaped with arms at each end of the bar. Ellipticals are ball-shaped, like a soccer ball, football, baseball, or anywhere in between. The fourth type, the irregular galaxy, has no obvious shape. No two of these are alike.

Shapes
The size of the central bulge and tightness of the arms around the center in spirals and barred spirals differ from galaxy to galaxy. Above left is spiral NGC 1232, and above right is barred spiral NGC 1300. Elliptical galaxy M32 is lower left, and the irregular-shaped Large Magellanic Cloud is lower right.

Milky Way

From inside the Milky Way we can look toward the galaxy's center. The concentration of stars makes a milky path of light across the night sky. Dark dust clouds hide more distant stars.

Home galaxy

The Sun is one of the 500 billion or so stars that make up the Milky Way galaxy. Astronomers believe it is a barred spiral, but it is difficult to see its overall shape from our position inside the galaxy. The Milky Way measures 100,000 light-years from side to side (one light-year is the distance light travels in one year—5.87 trillion mi.). Even the smallest galaxy is a few thousand light-years across, and the biggest is over one million light-years wide.

Cartwheel galaxy

Astronomers use numbers and location coordinates to identify galaxies. Some, however, are given unofficial names that make their way into regular usage. The unusual galaxy above is the Cartwheel—the result of two galaxies colliding.

Clusters

Galaxies exist in clusters, not randomly spread out through space. One cluster can contain tens, hundreds, or thousands of galaxies. The Coma cluster (above) has at least 1,000 bright galaxies. The Milky Way belongs to a cluster called the Local Group. This includes the Andromeda galaxy and the Small and Large Magellanic Clouds.

Life in space

Astronomers are often asked "Is there life in space?" It is a question no one can answer with certainty. The universe is enormous, and it would be surprising if Earth were the only place where life existed. But, for now, it is the only place where we know for certain that life exists. No life-form has been in touch with us on Earth, and we have not found any evidence of any living things, past or present, outside of Earth. Astronomers, however, are actively searching for signs of life in space.

Life on Earth

Studying life on Earth helps in the search for life in space. The elements needed for life as we know it—carbon, hydrogen, and oxygen—have been found throughout the universe. We also know that life can survive during extreme conditions. Deep in Earth's oceans, hot, chemical-rich water rushes up from volcanic regions, producing smokers (left). Bacteria, a simple, single-celled life-form, thrive on the sulfuric compounds inside these smokers, without oxygen and in boiling water.

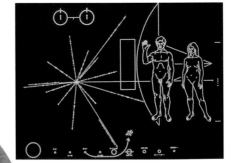

Messages from Earth

Space probes launched from Earth carry messages in case they are found by intelligent life. *Pioneers 10* and *11*, launched in 1972 and 1973, carried a plaque with a plan of the solar system and human figures. *Voyagers 1* and 2, launched in 1977, each carried a disk with sounds from Earth.

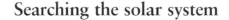

Searching the solar system

The planet Mars and Jupiter's moon Europa could be, or may have been in the past, home to primitive life-forms. Mars is cold now, and any water it has is frozen. It was hotter there in the past, and water once flowed across its surface. Simple life may have developed during that time. Two *Viking* probes landed on Mars in 1976 and tested the soil for signs of life. The results were inconclusive, but the search continues as new probes journey to Mars to make further investigations.

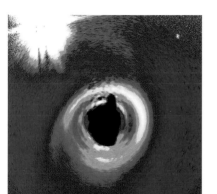

Extra-solar planets

It is likely that life exists on planets outside the solar system. Astronomers have known about young stars with dust rings—which are forming planets (left)—since 1984. The first extra-solar planet was found in 1995. More than 100 more are now known.

Life on Mars?

In 1996 a group of scientists mistakenly thought the microscopic, tubelike structures they were studying in a Martian rock were fossils of a primitive life-form.

Outside the solar system

Astronomers have been searching for intelligent life outside the solar system for more than 40 years. They use radio telescopes, such as the one at Parkes, Australia (right), to listen for signals that could have been sent to us deliberately or transmitted by chance. They are listening in to around 1,000 Sunlike stars, some of which we know have planets.

Small bang
The big bang was really a small explosion. But almost immediately after it the universe inflated. In a tiny fraction of a second it grew from smaller than an atom to bigger than a galaxy.

Beginning to end

The universe was created in an explosion that astronomers call the big bang around 13 billion years ago. All of the material in the universe today, as well as space and time, was created in that explosion. At first the material was only tiny particles, and these eventually produced today's stars and galaxies. The story of the universe, from big bang to the present, has been pieced together over the last 70 years or so. With each new observation or discovery astronomers learn more about our past and present and understand what the future could bring.

First elements
The very young universe, made up of incredibly tiny particles, was unimaginably hot and dense. Within three minutes of the big bang the temperature had dropped to 1.8 billion °F, and the first elements had formed. The universe was made up of around 77 percent hydrogen and 23 percent helium with a tiny amount of lithium.

Quasar

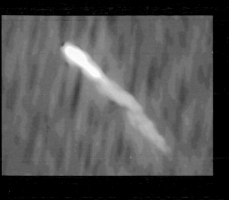

When astronomers look into the universe, they look back in time. Objects are so faraway that it takes their light millions or billions of years to reach us. Quasars (left) are the powerful cores of very remote galaxies. The first was identified by Dutch astronomer Maarten Schmidt in 1963.

First stars and galaxies

The universe cooled and became less dense as it grew, and around 300,000 years after the big bang it became transparent. Around 300 million years later the hydrogen and helium started to form into threads and then clouds surrounded by empty space. By the time the universe was around one billion years old these clouds were producing the first stars and galaxies.

Changing universe

The universe continues to change. Even now stars are forming, and galaxies are colliding and reshaping—and the whole universe is still cooling and expanding. Most astronomers believe that it will continue in this way until, in trillions of years, all the stars will have died, and the universe will be a cold, dark place.

Glossary

amateur someone who does something as a hobby. An amateur astronomer is someone who studies the stars and planets in their free time.

asteroid a small rock body orbiting the Sun. More than 90 percent are in the Main Belt between the orbits of Mars and Jupiter.

astronaut a man or woman who travels into space.

astronomer a person who studies the stars, planets, and other objects in space.

astronomy the study of everything in space—the solar system, the Milky Way, and everything outside the Milky Way.

atmosphere the layer of gases held around a planet or a moon by its gravity. A star's atmosphere is its layers of gas beyond its photosphere.

atom a tiny particle. An atom is the smallest particle of an element.

aurora a colorful display of light in the sky above Earth's polar regions.

billion one thousand million.

big bang the explosion that created the universe, space, and time around 13 billion years ago.

black hole the remains of a star that has collapsed in on itself. Its gravity is so strong nothing can get away from it.

brightness a measure of the light of a star. Astronomers measure brightness in two main ways. A scale of apparent brightness measures the brightness of a star seen from Earth. A scale of absolute brightness measures the real brightness of a star.

comet a small snow and dust body. Trillions of comets orbit the Sun beyond the planets. Together they form the Oort Cloud.

constellation a piece of sky whose bright stars form an imaginary pattern such a human or an animal.

cosmologist someone who studies the origin, evolution, and future of the universe.

crater a bowl-shaped hollow on the surface of a planet or moon, produced by a meteorite crashing into it.

dark matter the material in the universe that is invisible to us and has not yet been found. It makes up around 95 percent of the universe.

eclipse an effect achieved when one object in space is in the shadow of another. When the Earth's shadow falls on the Moon, it is a lunar eclipse. When the Moon covers the Sun and its shadow falls on Earth, it is a solar eclipse.

electromagnetic spectrum the range of energy waves that are given off by objects and that travel through space. The waves include light, radio waves, X rays, and infrared radiation.

element a basic substance of nature such as hydrogen or oxygen.

ellipse a two-dimensional shape. An ellipse is an elongated circle.

equator an imaginary line drawn around the middle of a planet or moon. It divides the top, northern half of the planet or moon from the bottom, southern half.

fossil the remains of something that lived in the past, such as a plant or an animal, which is preserved in a planet's surface material.

galaxy a vast number of stars, gas, and dust held together by gravity.

gravity a force of attraction found throughout the universe. The Sun's gravity pulls Earth, and Earth's pulls the Moon.

hemisphere one half of a planet or moon. The Northern Hemisphere is the half above the equator; the Southern Hemisphere is below.

Kuiper Belt the flat belt of icy rock objects that starts beyond the orbit of Neptune and reaches to the inner edge of the Oort Cloud.

latitude a measure of distance to the north or south of the Earth's equator. Latitude measurement is also used on other planets, moons, and the Sun.

light-year a measuring unit used by astronomers for distances outside the solar system. One light-year is the distance light travels in one year— 5.87 trillion mi.

luminosity the amount of light produced by a star.

mass the amount of material of which something is made.

meteor the streak of light produced by a meteoroid as it travels through Earth's atmosphere.

meteorite a space rock that lands on Earth or on another planet or a moon.

meteoroid a tiny piece of dust from a comet or asteroid that is no bigger than a grain of sand.

Milky Way the galaxy we live in. It is also the name of the path of stars in Earth's sky that is our view into the galaxy's disk.

moon a rock or rock and icy body that orbits a planet or an asteroid.

nebula a cloud of gas and dust in space. *See also* planetary nebula.

nuclear fusion the process by which elements inside a star produce other elements. For example, hydrogen atoms fuse to produce helium.

observatory a building or group of buildings that houses telescopes used for the observation of the stars and planets.

Oort Cloud the vast sphere of comets that surrounds the Sun and planets.

orbit the path one object takes around another, more massive, object. The Moon follows an orbit around Earth, and Earth orbits the Sun.

photosphere the outer, visible layer of the Sun, or any other star.

planet a large, spherical body made up of rock or gas that orbits the Sun or another star.

planetary nebula a type of star that consists of an expanding and colorful cloud of gas and dust, which has been ejected from a dying star.

professional someone who does something as their job. A professional astronomer is someone who is paid to study the stars and the planets.

pulsar a neutron star (a dense, collapsed star) that spins and sends pulses of energy into space.

quadrant a quarter of a circle. This is also the name for an astronomical instrument used mainly before the invention of the telescope, to measure the positions of the stars and planets in the sky.

quasar a very bright core of a distant galaxy. The name is a short form of quasi-stellar object.

radar a technique where radio waves are sent to an object and reflected back to measure the distance of the object. Astronomers use radar to map the surfaces of rocky bodies such as Venus.

reflector a telescope that uses mirrors to collect and focus light to form an image of a distant object.

refractor a telescope that uses lenses to collect and focus light to form an image of a distant object.

ring system a collection of rings surrounding a planet.

satellite an object held in orbit around a planet or moon by gravity. A telescope in orbit around Earth is a man-made satellite. The Moon is a natural satellite of Earth.

solar system the Sun and all the objects that orbit it. These include the nine planets, more than 100 moons, billions of space rocks, and trillions of comets.

space probe a type of spacecraft, also called a probe. A space probe is an unmanned craft sent to investigate objects in the solar system.

spectrum a spectrum of light is the rainbow band of colors produced when light is split. The plural of spectrum is spectra.

star a sphere of very hot and very luminous gas that produces energy by nuclear fusion.

supernova an old, massive star that has suddenly blown up.

telescope an instrument that uses lenses, mirrors, or a combination of the two to collect light from a distant object and form that light into an image. As well as light, telescopes can also collect other energy such as radio waves or X rays.

trillion one million million.

universe everything that exists—all of space and everything in it.

wavelength the distance between the peaks or dips in waves of electromagnetic radiation.

zodiac the band of 12 constellations that forms the backdrop to the path of the Sun, Moon, and planets as they move across the sky.

Index

Acknowledgments

The Publisher would like to thank the following for permission to reproduce their material. Every care has been taken to trace copyright holders. However, if there have been unintentional omissions or failure to trace copyright holders, we apologize and will, if informed, endeavor to make corrections in any future edition.

The Publisher would like to thank the following illustrators for their contributions to this book:
b = bottom, c = center, l = left, r = right, t = top
Jonathan Adams 13 br; **Julian Baker** 36; **Julian Baum** 23 tr, 27 tr, 31 tr, 33 b, 44–45, 49 r, 53 bl;
Mark Bristow 24–25, 38–39; **Mike Davis** cover; **Terry Gabbey (AFA O Ltd)** 9 t; **Alan Hancocks** 22–23 b,
34–35, 40–41, 50–51 br, 58–59; **Mike Roffe** 23 tc; **Mike White** 8–9 b; **Gareth Williams** 16–17, 48–49.

The Publishers would like to thank the following for supplying photographs for this book:
b = bottom, c = center, l = left, t = top
Pages: **4** bl SPL (Science Photo Library)/Magrath Photography; **4** br SPL/Frank Zullo; **5** cl Galaxy Picture Library/JPL,
5 tr SPL/Canada-France-Hawaii Telescope/Jean-Charles Cuillandre; **5** tc SPL/Dr Jean Lorre; **5** cr SPL/David Nunuk;
5 br SPL/Simon Fraser; **6-7** SPL/Dennis Milon/Allan Morton; **6** bl SPL/John Chumack; **7** tl David Malin Images/David Miller;
8 tr Werner Forman Archive/Private Collection; **9** tl Corbis/Danny Lehman; **10** tl SPL/Detlev van Ravenswaay;
10 c SPL/J-L. Charmet; **10** cr Bridgeman Art Library/British Library, London, UK; **11** tl SPL; **11** tr SPL/NASA/Space Telescope
Science Institute; **11** br Corbis/Bettman; **12** bl AKG Images; **12** bc Science and Society Picture Library/Science Museum;
13 tr SPL/David Parker; **13** c Science and Society Picture Library/Science Museum; **14** tr Corbis/Hulton-Deutsch Collection;
14 b SPL/David Parker; **15** tl Corbis/Hulton-Deutsch Collection; **15** bc Anglo-Australian Observatory/David Malin;
15 br Corbis/© Roger Ressmeyer; **16** cr Corbis/© Roger Ressmeyer; **17** tr European Southern Observatory/Pierre Kervella;
17 bl Bruce Coleman Collection/Astrofoto; **18** bl Royal Astronomical Society; **19** tr Corbis/Roger Ressmeyer;
19 c Corbis/Stephanie Maze; **19** cr Bruce Coleman Collection/European Southern Observatory; **19** br SPL/David Nunuk;
20 bl Corbis/© Roger Ressmeyer; **20** tr NASA/CXC/SAO; **21** tr SPL/IAP/Yannick Mellier; **22** tr SPL/NASA;
22 bl SPL/European Space Agency; **23** cl European Space Agency; **24** Science and Society Picture Library/Science Museum;
25 © National Maritime Museum, London; **26** b Trace Project/NASA; **26** tr Science and Society Picture Library/NASA;
27 bl SPL/Chris Madeley; **27** cr Science and Society Picture Library/Science Museum; **28** tr SPL/European Space Agency;
28 bl SPL/Dr Morley Read; **28** bcl Still Pictures/© Otto Hahn; **28** bcr Corbis/David Muench; **28** br SPL/Bernhard Edmaier;
29 tl Science and Society Picture Library/Science Museum; **29** br Corbis/© 1996, original image courtesy of NASA;
30 tr SPL/David Nunuk; **31** bl SPL/NASA; **32** tl Royal Astronomical Society; **33** tl Corbis/© Bettman; **34** bl NASA/NSSDC;
35 tr Corbis/Bettman; **36** tr SPL/NASA; **36** br Galaxy Picture Library/JPL; **36** bl Galaxy Picture Library/JPL; **37** tl Galaxy
Picture Library/Howard Miles; **37** cr SPL/Worldsat International Inc; **37** c SPL/Michael Abbey; **37** br Antarctic Search for
Meteorites Program/W.A. Cassidy; **38** cl Galaxy Picture Library/JPL; **39** tr Art Archive/Palazzo del Te Mantua/Dagli Orti (A);
39 cr Galaxy Picture Library/Robin Scagell; **39** br NASA/JPL/California Institute of Technology; **40** bl Galaxy Picture
Library/JPL; **40** cr SPL; **41** cl Galaxy Picture Library/STScI; **41** bl SPL/NASA; **41** cr Galaxy Picture Library/JPL; **41** br European
Southern Observatory; **42** tr SPL/NASA; **42** bl Galaxy Picture Library/JPL; **42** br Galaxy Picture Library/Calvin J. Hamilton;
43 tl SPL; **43** cl Galaxy Picture Library/OPM/Athéne Coustenis; **43** bl SPL/NASA; **43** br Galaxy Picture Library/JPL;
44 tr SPL/European Space Agency; **44** bl Bridgeman Art Library/Bridgeman Art Library Giraudon/Biblioteca Nacional, Madrid,
Spain; **45** tr SPL/John Chumack; **45** bc SPL/David Mclean; **46** tr © Institute of Astronomy, University of Cambridge;
46 bl SPL/National Optical Astronomy Observatories (NOAO); **47** tr Robert Gendler; **47** br SPL/Celestial Image Co;
48 © Bodleian Library, Oxford; **50** bl SPL/NASA/Space Telescope Science Institute; **50** tc es.geocities.com; **50** tr Lorand
Eöyvös University Gothard Astrophysical Observatory; **51** t SPL/Lynette Cook; **51** cl NASA/A Dupree (CfA) & R Cilliland
(STScI); **52** tr NASA/JPL/R Sahai; **52** tl NASA/ESA/HST/Garrelt Mellema (Leiden University); **52** bc SPL/NASA/Space
Telescope Science Institute; **53** tl SPL/NASA/Space Telescope Science Institute; **53** tr NOAO/AURA/NSF; **53** bc SPL/Robin
Scagell; **53** br NASA; **54** tl SPL; **54** cl European Southern Observatory (ESO); **54** c NSF/AURA/NOAO/Hilary Mathis;
54 bl NASA; **54** br NASA; **55** tr SPL/Dr Fred Espenak; **55** bc Galaxy Picture Library/STScI; **55** br SPL/Celestial Image Co;
56 l Galaxy Picture Library/NOAO/NURP/OAR; **56** bc Galaxy Picture Library/JPL; **56** br SPL/NASA; **57** tr Galaxy Picture
Library/NASA; **57** c NASA/M Clampin (STScI), H Ford (JHU), G Illingworth (UCO/Lick), J Krist (STScI), D Ardila (JHU),
D Golimowski (JHU), the ACS Science Team and ESA; **57** br SPL/Dr Seth Shostak; **58** tr SPL/David Parker; **59** tl Galaxy
Picture Library/Cavendish Laboratory; **59** tr Galaxy Picture Library/NASA/Space Telescope Science Institute; **Endpapers**
Royal Astronomical Society

Below is a list of useful web sites:
www.esa.int/export/esaCP/index.html (European Space Agency)
www.nasa.gov (NASA)
www.nmm.ac.uk (The Royal Observatory, Greenwich, England)
www.ras.org.uk (The Royal Astronomical Society)